A Puritan Theology
STUDY GUIDE

A Puritan Theology
STUDY GUIDE

Joel R. Beeke and
Mark Jones

Reformation Heritage Books
Grand Rapids, Michigan

Puritan Theology Study Guide
© 2016 by Joel R. Beeke and Mark Jones

Reformation Heritage Books
2965 Leonard St. NE
Grand Rapids, MI 49525
616-977-0889 / Fax 616-285-3246
orders@heritagebooks.org
www.heritagebooks.org

Printed in the United States of America
16 17 18 19 20 21/10 9 8 7 6 5 4 3 2 1

ISBN 978-1-60178-518-3

For additional Reformed literature, request a free book list from Reformation Heritage Books at the above regular or e-mail address.

Preface

Reading is one thing; reading well is another thing entirely. Reading well involves retention, understanding, and the ability to weigh the arguments and information. If you are going to invest the time and effort of reading a large book like *A Puritan Theology: Doctrine for Life*, then there is no point in dabbling. Hence, we offer a study guide for individuals and groups who desire to think deeply on these crucial subjects.

This study guide of *A Puritan Theology*, if used well, will require considerable work by the reader. But where there is great effort there will usually be great benefit. We venture to say that answering the questions in this booklet will make one not only a good theologian, but also a good historical theologian.

A Puritan Theology aims to present you with a basic Puritan systematic theology that addresses more than fifty areas of teaching sound doctrine where the Puritans excel. It also includes eight chapters on specific areas in which the Puritans brought their theology to bear on practical, daily life.

Since each chapter of our book stands on its own, it goes without saying that not all of the questions need to be answered, just as all of the chapters in the book do not need to be read. Readers can begin from the front and read through to the end. Or they can decide on a section (loci) in the book and work away at Puritan Soteriology, for example. Or, if they have difficulty reading theology, they could read the last section first on "Theology in Practice," and then have their appetite whetted to go back to the beginning and work their way through the book. There's lots of freedom here.

But whatever you do, prayerfully approach your studies, and use this time to learn. To students of theology, keep in mind the following advice from the Prince of the Puritans, John Owen: "Wherever fear and caution have not infused the student's heart, God is despised. His pleasure is only to dwell in hearts which tremble at His Word. Light or frivolous perusal of the Scriptures is a sickness of soul which leads on to the death of atheism."

Moreover, according to Owen, it is imperative, for the good of the student, "that he carefully weigh up and monitor what progress he is making: (1) in all of the truth which he is busy digging out of the Word, and (2) in acceptable worship of God.

Let the latter be the first and main purpose of all his studies and meditations in the Holy Scriptures.... Our studies are useless if they do not teach us about our own standing before God and our Lord Jesus."

Lastly, all of our study should be "preceded, accompanied, and closed by continuous and heart-felt prayer. This is the most effectual means ordained of God for discovering that heavenly wisdom for which we are seeking."

Many thanks to Michael Dewalt and Paul Smalley for their assistance on this guide. We trust this guide, the book, and the advice of Owen above will help readers of *A Puritan Theology* to grow in the grace and knowledge of their Savior, Jesus Christ.

—Joel R. Beeke and Mark Jones

A Puritan Theology
STUDY GUIDE

Chapter 1

1. According to Stephen Charnock, how can fallen man know God without Christ? What ten attributes of God does Charnock assert to be recognizable to non-believers by the light of nature?

2. According to John Owen, what is the threefold meaning of *the word of God*, and what does each Greek term mean?

3. According to Owen, what makes Scripture divine and infallible? How did God reveal Himself to the writers of Scripture so that we have the very Word of God today?

4. Why was the doctrine of covenant theology crucial for understanding supernatural theology in Puritan thought?

5. What is the source of all supernatural theology? How does this source reveal God not only to men but to angels as well?

6. Explain Thomas Goodwin's position on Adam's natural theology, or knowledge of God, before the fall.

Chapter 2

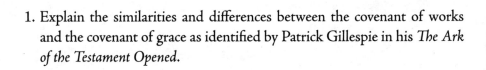

1. Explain the similarities and differences between the covenant of works and the covenant of grace as identified by Patrick Gillespie in his *The Ark of the Testament Opened.*

2. How did the Puritans view Christ as the major principle of interpretation?

3. What is the *sensus literalis,* and how is this principle foundational for biblical interpretation?

4. What is the difference between typology and allegory when it comes to interpreting the Old Testament?

5. What are the roles of logical consequence and reason in interpreting Scripture?

6. Explain the difference between the analogy of faith (*analogia fidei*) and the analogy of Scripture (*analogia Scripturae*).

Chapter 3

———————————— ❖ ————————————

1. What is Ramism?

2. What was the fundamental unity between John Calvin and William Ames's understanding of the Godward life?

3. Does Ames's view of the human will align with traditional Reformed doctrine or is it Arminian in nature? Explain.

4. How did Ames explain covenant theology and use it to structure his teaching on the fall and redemption of man?

5. Describe the organization and content of Ames's ethics.

6. In what ways did Ames's life exemplify how those who seek to live a pious life will suffer?

Chapter 4

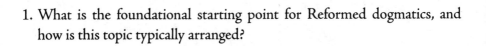

1. What is the foundational starting point for Reformed dogmatics, and how is this topic typically arranged?

2. If God is immutable, why does Scripture speak of Him repenting?

3. According to Charnock, how does Christ's suffering and death manifest both God's holiness and goodness?

4. Why does the division of God's attributes reflect our weakness in understanding God?

5. Describe Stephen Charnock's view of the influential omnipresence of God.

6. Explain why "middle knowledge" is inconsistent with Charnock's doctrine of God's comprehensive knowledge (omniscience).

Chapter 5

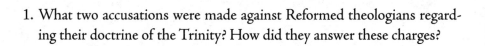

1. What two accusations were made against Reformed theologians regarding their doctrine of the Trinity? How did they answer these charges?

2. How did the Puritans describe the mutual communion of persons in the Trinity?

3. What is the doctrine of double procession of the Spirit, and why is it important for understanding the relationship between the Father and the Son?

4. The Socinians claimed that the Son's deity implies division in the essence of God. Explain how the eternal generation of the Son refutes that claim.

5. What was the debate among the Reformed regarding the Son's aseity (self-existence)?

6. What did Thomas Goodwin and John Owen teach on the principle *opera trinitatis ad extra sunt indivisa?*

Chapter 6

1. According to John Owen, why did God reveal Himself as the Trinity?

2. What did Owen mean by communion or fellowship with God? Why is this important for a true understanding of God?

3. What Scriptures did Owen see as proof that the believer has distinct communion with each person of the Trinity?

4. How do the saints have communion with the Father, both in receiving from Him and returning to Him?

5. What are the two kinds of grace in Christ? How did Owen explain communion with the Son of God in terms of each kind?

6. How did Owen relate communion with the Spirit to communion with the Father and the Son?

7. Explain the three distinct ways that John Owen believed we should respond to the Spirit.

Chapter 7

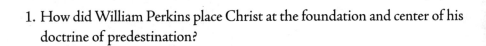

1. How did William Perkins place Christ at the foundation and center of his doctrine of predestination?

2. According to Perkins, what are the means by which God executes His decree of predestination?

3. What is the process of effectual calling? What is the product of effectual calling?

4. What differences did Perkins set between election and reprobation?

5. How did Perkins relate preaching to predestination?

6. Define supralapsarianism. Explain how Perkins addresses the objection that supralapsarianism makes God the author of sin.

7. Describe the monopleuric view of the covenant of grace and the dipleuric view of the covenant of grace. Explain how conversion is the point of reconciliation between the monopleuric and dipleuric aspects of covenant theology.

Chapter 8

1. What is eternal justification?

2. What are the "three sorts of works that accomplish our salvation," according to Thomas Goodwin? How does he relate each of the three to justification?

3. How do the doctrines of union with Christ and eternal justification relate to each other?

4. What did Goodwin teach about the spiritual status of the elect before faith in Christ?

5. What was the difference between Goodwin's understanding of eternal justification and Johannes Maccovius's understanding?

6. Why would those who believe in eternal justification be charged with antinomianism?

7. Did John Gill and Alexander Comrie correctly understand Maccovius on justification? Why or why not?

Chapter 9

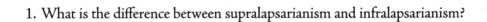

1. What is the difference between supralapsarianism and infralapsarianism?

2. What was the reason for the debate about the phrase "in Christ" in Ephesians 1:4? What position did Goodwin take?

3. What is the difference between election and predestination (Ephesians 1:4–5)? How does it affect one's understanding of supralapsarianism?

4. Why is it important that Christ Himself was predestined?

5. What is the ultimate end of predestination with respect to Christ? What is the end of predestination with respect to God's elect people?

6. What makes Goodwin's doctrine of supralapsarianism "Christological"?

Chapter 10

1. How would you summarize a Puritan definition of providence?

2. What is one of the greatest blessings of providence, according to John Flavel?

3. How does God's providence relate to man's sinning?

4. If God is providential, why do His people suffer?

5. Describe William Ames's understanding on Romans 11:36 as it relates to God's providence.

6. Describe the unorthodox belief held by the Socinians regarding the providence of God.

7. How did the Puritans encourage submission to painful providences?

Chapter 11

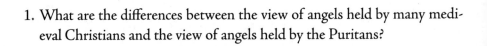

1. What are the differences between the view of angels held by many medieval Christians and the view of angels held by the Puritans?

2. How does the doctrine of election pertain to angels?

3. What did Samuel Willard teach about the nature of angels? How did he compare them to God?

4. What does the Westminster Larger Catechism teach about the history of angels?

5. Richard Godbeer distinguishes between *supplicative* and *manipulative* spirituality. Define these terms.

6. Considering the office and present work of angels, describe how angels serve people.

7. How did the Puritans guard against overmuch speculation and attention to angels?

Chapter 12

1. Can Satan and demons be redeemed?

2. According to Jonathan Edwards and Thomas Goodwin, what was the reason Satan rebelled?

3. List three devices of Satan and their remedies.

4. According to Edward Reynolds, what titles does Scripture give to Satan? What does each mean?

5. Why did the Puritans speak more about the doctrine of demons than the doctrine of angels?

6. List the four points that Isaac Ambrose expounded from Ephesians 6:12 concerning the power of demonic angels.

7. How did Jonathan Edwards differ from popular Puritan commentators on the interpretation of Isaiah 14 and Ezekiel 28?

Chapter 13

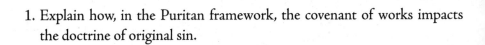

1. Explain how, in the Puritan framework, the covenant of works impacts the doctrine of original sin.

2. How did the Puritans argue from Scripture that Adam's guilt was immediately imputed to mankind?

3. What Puritan theologian wrote best on remaining sin in believers? Which wrote best on reigning sin in unbelievers?

4. Describe the effects of the fall upon man's mind in terms of both natural defects and spiritual defects.

5. According to Anthony Burgess and John Owen, how does regeneration affect original sin?

6. Describe John Owen's understanding on Christian freedom from sin's domination.

7. This chapter suggests that "the real issue that separates Reformed theology from other theological traditions" is the doctrine of sin. Why might this be so?

Chapter 14

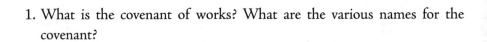

1. What is the covenant of works? What are the various names for the covenant?

2. In what sense did some theologians view the tree of life as sacramental, and others as typical?

3. How could Adam and Eve have sinned if they were made "very good"? Did Adam have the ability to stand or was there a defect in his design?

4. How did the Puritans explain that God is not to be blamed for man's fall?

5. According to the divines, how was grace present in the covenant of works?

6. What is "good and necessary consequence" and how does it function in arguments for the covenant of works?

7. Describe the Puritan understanding of the law of nature, in regards to man being created in the *imago Dei*.

Chapter 15

1. What is the covenant of redemption?

2. How did the Puritans differ from each other regarding the necessity of satisfying God's justice?

3. What eight promises were made to Christ in the covenant of redemption?

4. What is the Holy Spirit's role in the covenant of redemption?

5. Explain the covenant of redemption in the context of God's justice.

6. Explain Christ's subordination to the Father in terms of a covenant of redemption.

7. How is the covenant of redemption related to the covenant of grace?

Chapter 16

1. What is the covenant of grace?

2. According to Francis Roberts, why was the Noahic covenant an administration of the covenant of grace?

3. According to the Puritans, how did the covenant with Abraham reveal more of God's grace?

4. According to Roberts, William Gouge, and John Ball, how did the covenant with David manifest Christ in His three offices?

5. What is the "captivity covenant"?

6. How are the covenants in the Old Testament fulfilled in the new covenant?

7. Describe the Roman Catholic Church's position regarding the promise of the "seed of the woman" (Genesis 3:15) and compare it to the Puritan/Reformed view of the text.

Chapter 17

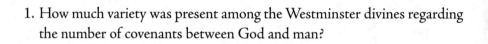

1. How much variety was present among the Westminster divines regarding the number of covenants between God and man?

2. What points of agreement among Reformed theologians on the old covenant did John Owen highlight?

3. What is the dichotomous view of God's covenants?

4. How was the understanding of the Lutheran divines on the Mosaic covenant different from that of the Reformed divines?

5. How did many Reformed theologians argue that the Sinai covenant was part of the covenant of grace?

6. What is the trichotomous view of God's covenants? In what sense was the covenant of Moses considered a "subservient covenant"?

Chapter 18

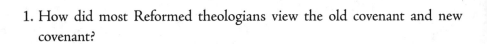

1. How did most Reformed theologians view the old covenant and new covenant?

2. What theologians adopted a trichotomist view of the historical covenants?

3. Was John Owen's view of the covenants dichotomous or trichotomous? Explain.

4. Why did Owen prefer to speak of the *promise* of grace with respect to God's dealings with men prior to Christ's death, instead of the covenant of grace or new covenant?

5. Why, according to Owen, is the Mosaic covenant not a republication of the covenant of works but a renewal of the moral law?

6. What positive functions did Owen see in the old covenant?

Chapter 19

1. What two theological controversies shaped the Puritan discussion of whether the covenant of grace is one-sided or two-sided?

2. Peter Bulkeley and Francis Roberts argued that the covenant of grace must be two-sided. Explain their argument.

3. How did John Flavel use the distinctions of meritorious conditions versus non-meritorious conditions and essential conditions versus instrumental conditions to clarify how faith is a condition for justification?

4. Explain the Reformed teaching (against the Lutherans and Romanists) that good works are necessary not for justification, but as the way to salvation and glory.

5. According to Thomas Goodwin and John Owen, how will God glorify Himself by judging people according to their works on the last day?

6. How do articles 13–15 of A New Confession (1654) declare evangelical obedience to be a necessary aspect of salvation for God's people who are in covenant with Him?

7. How did John Davenant explain that good works are required of those who are already justified and yet avoid the errors of the Roman Catholic Church?

Chapter 20

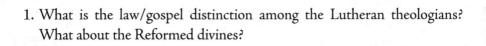

1. What is the law/gospel distinction among the Lutheran theologians? What about the Reformed divines?

2. What is an Antinomian? Why is it difficult to define antinomianism?

3. Describe Samuel Rutherford's view on what he called the "new heresy of the Antinomians" who deny "a conditional gospel."

4. What criticisms did Rutherford use against "Antinomians" for teaching that there are no conditions for salvation in the covenant?

5. What did Anthony Burgess teach about the place of law, works, and repentance in the covenant of grace?

6. How did Thomas Goodwin define the gospel so that it included both Christ's works *for* us and His works *in* us?

Chapter 21

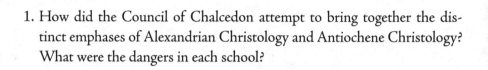

1. How did the Council of Chalcedon attempt to bring together the distinct emphases of Alexandrian Christology and Antiochene Christology? What were the dangers in each school?

2. In terms of Christology, what do the Reformed mean by "the finite cannot contain the infinite"?

3. What is the doctrine of the hypostatic union?

4. What did John Arrowsmith say about whether Christ assumed our infirmities when He took human nature?

5. How would you summarize what the Westminster Confession says about the communication of properties in Christ?

6. According to John Owen and Thomas Goodwin, what is the role of the Spirit in the human holiness of Christ and miracles performed by Christ?

7. Why is it crucial to understand the doctrine of the person of Christ in order to understand the work of Christ?

Chapter 22

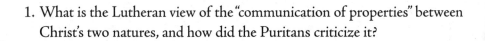

1. What is the Lutheran view of the "communication of properties" between Christ's two natures, and how did the Puritans criticize it?

2. What did John Owen teach about Christ's office as prophet?

3. According to the Puritans, what are the two main functions of Christ as priest? How are these functions related to each other?

4. List the nine privileges God bestowed upon Christ as the God-man that are necessary for establishing His spiritual kingdom and rule as King.

5. How did Edward Reynolds explain the significance of Christ's exaltation with respect to His divine nature and human nature?

6. Why did Richard Sibbes consider it "a sweet meditation" to reflect on Christ's humiliation and exaltation?

Chapter 23

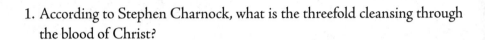

1. According to Stephen Charnock, what is the threefold cleansing through the blood of Christ?

2. Explain what Charnock meant by saying believers "are not righteous before God by an inherent, but by an imputed righteousness." How is such imputation possible?

3. How did Isaac Ambrose defend from Scripture the doctrine that Christ's death was a satisfaction of divine justice?

4. According to Ambrose, what is the difference between faith in Christ and a merely emotional response to His sufferings?

5. Explain how the blood of Christ not only justifies but also sanctifies.

6. How did the Puritans believe that the blood of Christ promotes piety?

Chapter 24

1. How can Christ's prayers to His Father encourage us in light of the fact that Christ interceded as the only Mediator? Why can we also learn from Christ's prayers how ordinary men and women can pray to God?

2. According to Burgess, what does the scope of Christ's prayer—particularly, for whom He prayed—imply about those for whom Christ died?

3. According to Burgess, what are five comforting truths about Christ's exaltation?

4. Why is Christ's work as Mediator a strong foundation for prayer with peace and faith?

5. If God is sovereign and Christ's prayer is all in all, what need is there to pray?

6. List the points Burgess made in explaining why all of our prayers are to be heavenly-minded.

7. Why did Burgess believe that prayers should contain "arguments"? What are some examples he gave of biblical "arguments" in prayer?

Chapter 25

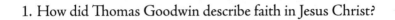

1. How did Thomas Goodwin describe faith in Jesus Christ?

2. According to Goodwin, what problem does Christ's passing into heaven pose for our faith? What is the solution?

3. How can Christ be tender-hearted toward believers now that He is glorified and freed from all earthly pain and cares?

4. What did Goodwin find in John 13 through John 20 that indicated Christ will always be compassionate towards His people?

5. How did Goodwin prove Christ's compassion from what we know of each person in the Trinity?

6. What are the four applications to believers that Goodwin gives in *The Heart of Christ*? How do they apply to your life?

Chapter 26

1. Why did the Puritans love God's promises?

2. According to Edward Leigh, what are the three ways the Word teaches us? How are they different?

3. What is the difference between legal promises and evangelical promises? Absolute promises and conditional promises?

4. According to Andrew Gray, what are eight ways in which the promises are exceedingly precious?

5. What ten benefits of believing God's promises are offered by Gray?

6. What was the best way of applying the promises of God, according to William Spurstowe?

7. What did Leigh teach about how to pray God's promises?

Chapter 27

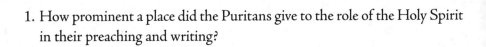

1. How prominent a place did the Puritans give to the role of the Holy Spirit in their preaching and writing?

2. How did the Puritans prove the deity and personality of the Holy Spirit, as opposed to the errors that the Spirit is not God or is an impersonal power?

3. How did Thomas Goodwin argue that believers should treat the Spirit's work as equally important to the work of Christ?

4. Explain how the Spirit's work was instrumental not only in Christ's state of humiliation but also in His state of exaltation.

5. How did the Puritans interpret Zechariah 12:10 with regard to the Spirit's work in prayer?

6. How did the Puritans relate the Spirit's "groanings" (Romans 8:26–27) to the prayers of God's people?

7. How did the Puritans view the "inner light" teachings of the early Quakers?

Chapter 28

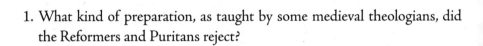

1. What kind of preparation, as taught by some medieval theologians, did the Reformers and Puritans reject?

2. What did John Flavel believe was generally needed to awaken sinners to their need for Christ?

3. How did Flavel distinguish between preparatory conviction of sin and saving conversion to Christ?

4. How have scholars often set Calvin against many of the Puritans regarding preparation for conversion? What has further research shown?

5. What errors did some Puritans fall into regarding preparation?

6. How is the Reformed view of preparation different from the Roman Catholic teaching?

7. How does the three-fold pattern of Paul's Epistle to the Romans support the idea of preparation by conviction of sin for saving faith?

Chapter 29

1. What did the Reformers and Puritans mean by "regeneration" in its broadest sense? In its narrow sense, how did regeneration relate to effectual calling?

2. What are several reasons given by Stephen Charnock why regeneration is necessary?

3. What were the views of regeneration held by Flacius Illyricus, the Socinians, and the Arminians?

4. How did the Puritans compare regeneration to reformation of manners and moral persuasion?

5. What role did the Puritans give to the Word in regeneration?

6. What are some signs of regeneration, according to Ezekiel Hopkins?

Chapter 30

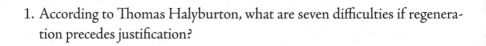

1. According to Thomas Halyburton, what are seven difficulties if regeneration precedes justification?

2. What is Peter Bulkeley and Halyburton's doctrine of the threefold union with Christ?

3. Why did the Puritans see union with Christ as the greatest and most fundamental of all spiritual blessings?

4. According to Thomas Goodwin and John Owen, how does regeneration relate to union with Christ?

5. How did Herman Witsius distinguish between a real but passive union with Christ and a mutual union with Christ?

6. How did the Puritans relate union with Christ to communion with Christ?

7. How did William Lyford use the doctrine of union with Christ to explain how His righteousness can be imputed to believers?

Chapter 31

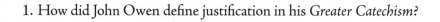

1. How did John Owen define justification in his *Greater Catechism?*

2. What did Owen teach regarding the nature of justifying faith?

3. How does such faith function for our justification, according to Owen? How was his view different from Richard Baxter's view of faith as the formal cause of our justification?

4. What is the Roman Catholic doctrine of double justification? Did Owen agree?

5. How did Calvin understand imputation? Was Owen's view significantly different?

6. How did Owen ground the imputation of Christ's righteousness upon His office as surety, established in the covenant of redemption?

7. How did Owen explain imputation by comparison to Adam?

Chapter 32

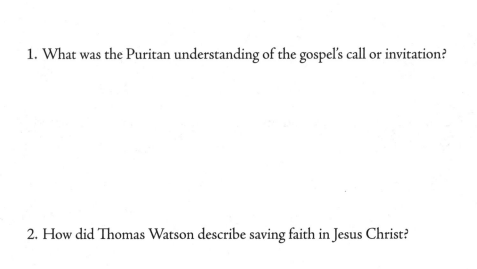

1. What was the Puritan understanding of the gospel's call or invitation?

2. How did Thomas Watson describe saving faith in Jesus Christ?

3. According to John Bunyan, why is the doctrine of God's effectual call inseparable from absolute or unconditional promises?

4. According to Stephen Charnock, what is the difference between conversion and regeneration?

5. According to Richard Baxter, what are the hindrances of conversion? What are some examples of hindrances you experienced in your conversion?

6. Describe the Puritans' understanding on the inability of fallen man to respond to God, and how God overcomes it.

Chapter 33

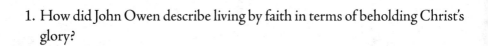

1. How did John Owen describe living by faith in terms of beholding Christ's glory?

2. How does the Westminster Shorter Catechism describe sanctification and its benefits (together with justification and adoption)?

3. How did the Puritans link our sanctification to God's holiness?

4. How is the Puritan practice of sanctification trinitarian?

5. What is the difference between the doctrine of mortification and the doctrine of vivification? Why are these doctrines so foundational and important to sanctification?

6. Explain the various spiritual disciplines the Puritans believed lead to *Christlikeness*.

7. Explain the connection the Puritans made between *holiness* and *vocation*.

Chapter 34

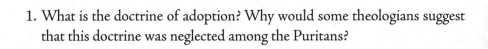

1. What is the doctrine of adoption? Why would some theologians suggest that this doctrine was neglected among the Puritans?

2. How did Stephen Marshall see adoption as comprehensive of our entire salvation?

3. How did the Puritans distinguish between regeneration and adoption?

4. What contributions did the Westminster Standards make to the doctrine of adoption?

5. According to William Ames, what are the four differences between human and divine adoption?

6. What are the six marks of adoption, according to William Perkins?

7. What responsibilities does adoption place on children of God?

Chapter 35

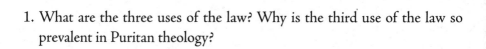

1. What are the three uses of the law? Why is the third use of the law so prevalent in Puritan theology?

2. What is antinomianism? Why did the Roman Catholic Church charge the Reformers with this?

3. How did Samuel Bolton explain that a Christian is under grace yet under the moral law for obedience?

4. In what six ways is the Christian still "under the law," according to William Fenner?

5. What five rules did George Downame give for applying each of the Ten Commandments?

6. Describe the debate between the Reformers and the Roman Catholics regarding the sufficiency of the law for moral instruction.

Chapter 36

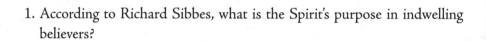

1. According to Richard Sibbes, what is the Spirit's purpose in indwelling believers?

2. How can one know he has the Holy Spirit in him?

3. What is Sibbes's understanding of being sealed with the Spirit? How did Owen disagree with him on this?

4. According to Sibbes, what are the three kinds of Christians? Is this distinction biblical? Explain.

5. How did Sibbes describe the Spirit's ministry of comfort?

6. What was Sibbes's understanding on grieving the Spirit?

Chapter 37

1. How did William Perkins employ the condition and unconditional dimensions of the covenant of grace to establish assurance of salvation?

2. How did Perkins use the image of an instrument or hand to describe how faith relates to Jesus Christ?

3. What is Perkins "five degrees in the work of faith"? What is the difference, according to Perkins, between weak faith and strong faith?

4. List Perkins's three grounds of assurance.

5. How did Perkins use the practical syllogism to illustrate how a conscience finds assurance?

6. What marks of saving grace did Perkins find in 1 John?

7. Describe the various signs of a hypocrite, according to William Perkins.

Chapter 38

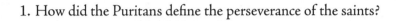

1. How did the Puritans define the perseverance of the saints?

2. How can we believe in the doctrine of perseverance, yet hold that there are apostates who leave the faith?

3. Opponents suggested that this doctrine gives rise to antinomianism and neglects human responsibility; how did John Owen respond to this charge?

4. How did the Puritans ground perseverance in the Father's electing love and covenant?

5. How did they ground perseverance in Christ's work and our union with Him by the Holy Spirit?

6. Why, according to the Puritans, is perseverance necessary?

7. Describe the means of perseverance according to the Puritans.

Chapter 39

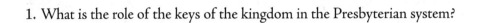

1. What is the role of the keys of the kingdom in the Presbyterian system?

2. How did the Presbyterian system understand the difference between the visible and invisible church?

3. What are the distinguishing marks between the Presbyterian and congregational forms of governments?

4. What is the scriptural basis for church discipline in the congregational system?

5. Describe John Owen's position on the visible "catholic" church.

6. According to Owen, what does congregational consent look like in a congregational church and how democratic could it be?

7. Explain the various defects some Presbyterian saw in the Congregationalist rejection of authoritative synods.

Chapter 40

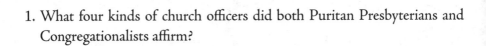

1. What four kinds of church officers did both Puritan Presbyterians and Congregationalists affirm?

2. How can an ecclesiology be trinitarian, according to Thomas Goodwin and John Owen?

3. What did William Ames mean by his distinction between extraordinary and ordinary ministers?

4. What responsibilities did Owen say belonged to a pastor?

5. How did Owen and Goodwin define the office of a teacher as distinct from a pastor?

6. Upon what biblical basis did Owen distinguish elders into pastors and ruling elders? How were these offices different?

7. Describe Owen and Goodwin's understanding of church deacons.

Chapter 41

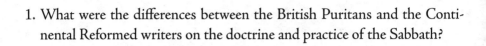

1. What were the differences between the British Puritans and the Continental Reformed writers on the doctrine and practice of the Sabbath?

2. When was the Sabbath instituted, according to John Owen? Why does it matter?

3. How did God distinguish the Ten Commandments from the other laws He gave to Israel?

4. According to Owen, why is only Scripture sufficient for worship?

5. What did John Calvin believe about any form of worship "not expressly sanctioned" by God's Word?

6. Describe the difference John Owen saw between the role of worship in the Old and New covenants.

Chapter 42

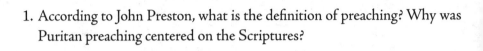

1. According to John Preston, what is the definition of preaching? Why was Puritan preaching centered on the Scriptures?

2. How did Puritan preaching differ from that of non-Puritans in the Church of England?

3. What did the Puritans mean by "plain" preaching?

4. What are the six applications of preaching given by the Westminster divines?

5. What seven categories of listeners did William Perkins say should guide the preacher in making application?

6. What seven adverbs did the Westminster divines say should characterize preaching?

7. Give three examples of what the modern preacher can learn about preaching from the Puritans.

Chapter 43

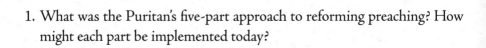

1. What was the Puritan's five-part approach to reforming preaching? How might each part be implemented today?

2. Explain what the words *experimental* and *discriminatory* mean with respect to Puritan preaching.

3. What were the three reasons the Puritans were passionate about preaching?

4. How did the Puritans' passion for preaching spring from their heart for Christ?

5. Why did the Puritans love the work of preaching itself?

6. According to Thomas Manton, what are four ways to help weak Christians come to stronger faith?

7. Why was a love for people so essential to Puritan preaching?

Chapter 44

1. What about John Bunyan's life made his preaching so hearty and effective?

2. What are three kinds of spiritual experience that shaped Bunyan's preaching? How do these enliven any preacher?

3. How did Bunyan use imaginative forms to engage his listeners?

4. How did Bunyan use direct appeals and pleading to engage his listeners?

5. What did Bunyan mean when he said he "preached what I saw and felt"? How did this affect his preaching?

6. Describe Bunyan's preaching of Jesus Christ. How did this honor Christ?

Chapter 45

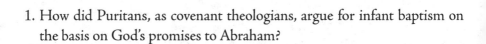

1. How did Puritans, as covenant theologians, argue for infant baptism on the basis on God's promises to Abraham?

2. How did Philip Cary base his view of Genesis 17 on his unconditional view of the covenant of grace?

3. In what sense did Cary believe that Abraham and Moses were under two covenants at the same time?

4. How did John Flavel use the idea of a covenant as a "mutual compact or agreement" to argue against Cary?

5. What seven points did Flavel make about the relationship between the covenant of works and the covenant of grace? How do they show the complexity of the distinction between the law and promise in Reformed covenant theology?

6. How did Benjamin Keach respond to Flavel's arguments?

7. How does this debate illustrate the differing views of the covenant of grace held by Paedobaptists and Baptists in the late seventeenth century?

Chapter 46

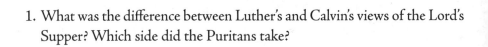

1. What was the difference between Luther's and Calvin's views of the Lord's Supper? Which side did the Puritans take?

2. What arguments did William Perkins bring against the transubstantial and sacrificial teachings of the Roman Catholic Church on the Lord's Supper?

3. How did the Puritans understand Christ's presence in the Supper?

4. Explain the various qualifications for admission to the Lord's Supper, according to the Puritans.

5. What are the three hindrances to the Lord's Supper? How can these hindrances be prevented?

6. What are the benefits of the Lord's Supper?

Chapter 47

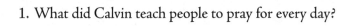

1. What did Calvin teach people to pray for every day?

2. What six beliefs of the Puritans fueled their prayers for world missions?

3. How did Jonathan Edwards argue for prayer based on biblical promises about Christ's kingdom?

4. What did the Westminster divines teach churches to pray for on a regular basis?

5. How does Matthew Henry's *Method for Prayer* encourage prayers for missions?

6. How has singing the Psalms kept world missions in the minds and hearts of Reformed Christians?

Chapter 48

1. What are some challenges historians face when dealing with the study of Puritan eschatology?

2. How did the historical and political events of the time influence how the Puritans developed their eschatology?

3. What were common Puritan views of the millennium, the Antichrist, the future of the Jews, and the future of the church?

4. How did Puritans such as John Cotton and John Winthrop express the place of New England in their eschatological hope?

5. Describe the eschatology of Cotton Mather.

6. How did the hope of Puritan eschatology influence their lives in practical ways?

Chapter 49

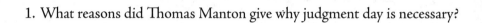

1. What reasons did Thomas Manton give why judgment day is necessary?

2. How did Manton explain Christ's act of judging in terms of His divine and human natures?

3. To what seven types of people will Christ bring terror to as Judge? Christ will bring comfort to those who do what four things?

4. According to Manton, how will judgment according to works reveal God's glory?

5. Explain the threefold nature of God's justice according to Manton?

6. What did Manton teach about the judgment of believers in Christ according to their works, particularly in light of their justification by faith alone?

7. What did Manton teach about God's punishment of the wicked?

Chapter 50

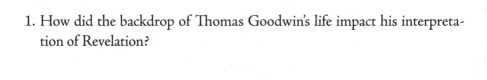

1. How did the backdrop of Thomas Goodwin's life impact his interpretation of Revelation?

2. What is the historicist reading of Revelation? How did Goodwin divide Revelation into sections?

3. Where did Goodwin see the Reformation in the sequence of Revelation?

4. How did Goodwin interpret Revelation 11?

5. What is the threefold glory of Christ, and what was its correlation to Goodwin's eschatology?

6. What was Goodwin's understanding of the millennium?

Chapter 51

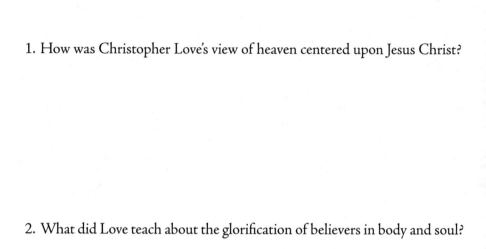

1. How was Christopher Love's view of heaven centered upon Jesus Christ?

2. What did Love teach about the glorification of believers in body and soul?

3. What five arguments did Love offer that believers will recognize each other in heaven?

4. How did Love define what hell is?

5. Why did Love believe that God is just in damning men to hell forever?

6. What did Love teach about the torments of hell?

Chapter 52

1. What does it mean to say that the Puritans had "a pilgrim mentality"?

2. What did the preface to the Geneva Bible say about the Scriptures?

3. What is biblical piety? What means did the Puritans use to promote it?

4. Why did the Puritans believe that the worship of the church was pure only if it followed God's Word and did not add humanly invented practices?

5. What is the Puritan understanding of spiritual warfare?

6. How did the Puritans exemplify a disciplined, methodical approach to life?

7. How did the Puritans' focus on heaven and hell help them to live as pilgrims?

Chapter 53

1. How did the Puritans admonish fathers to rule their homes with mercy?

2. Why did the Puritans believe it was crucial for parents to live with integrity at home and guard the purity of their homes?

3. In the 1677 covenant of the church of Dorchester, Massachusetts, what did the church members commit themselves to do in their families?

4. How did the Puritans see Abraham (Genesis 18:19) and Jacob (Genesis 35:1–15) as examples of family worship?

5. What did William Perkins teach as the two main branches of the duty of family worship? What Scriptures did he quote to support this teaching?

6. What motivations did the Puritans press upon people to practice family worship?

Chapter 54

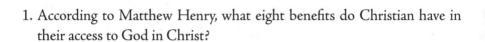

1. According to Matthew Henry, what eight benefits do Christian have in their access to God in Christ?

2. What motivations and instructions did Henry give for beginning each day with God?

3. How did Henry counsel us to spend every day with God even when we are working in our various vocations?

4. What did Henry believe should be in prayer "the guide of your desires and the ground of your expectations"? How did he build a "method" of prayer on this?

5. Described the pattern of kinds of prayers that Henry followed in this method.

6. How did Henry warn against reading words as prayers without meditating on them?

Chapter 55

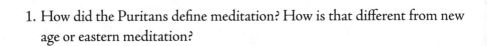

1. How did the Puritans define meditation? How is that different from new age or eastern meditation?

2. What is the difference between occasional meditation and deliberate meditation?

3. According to the Puritans, what are seven reasons we need meditation?

4. What advice did the Puritans give on how to plan and prepare for meditation?

5. Summarize in brief points the guidelines on the actual process of meditation.

6. Looking over the list of subjects of meditation, which subjects were mentioned most often among the Puritans? Why might this be so?

7. Which of the obstacles to meditation is most relevant to you? How did the Puritans address that obstacle?

Chapter 56

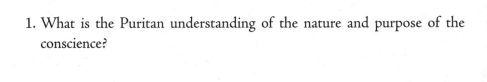

1. What is the Puritan understanding of the nature and purpose of the conscience?

2. What metaphors did the Puritans use to describe the conscience?

3. According to the Puritans, what role does conscience fulfill in the soul?

4. What are six ways in which the conscience has been corrupted by the fall? How does each harm the soul of man?

5. How is the conscience awakened by preaching?

6. Why must Scripture inform the conscience?

7. How can the gospel heal the conscience?

Chapter 57

1. What is casuistry in the Reformed (and Lutheran) tradition?

2. Describe how pastoral casuistry emerged among the early Puritans like Richard Greenham, Richard Rogers, and others.

3. How did William Perkins further develop Puritan casuistry?

4. Describe William Ames's book, *Conscience with the Power and Cases Thereof.*

5. What are six reasons Tim Keller gives for studying Puritan writings to learn biblical counseling?

6. What are some lessons we can learn from the Puritans about counseling?

Chapter 58

1. How did the Puritans define Christian zeal? What are its characteristics?

2. According to Samuel Ward, what are the three types of false zeal?

3. What did the Puritans say about the necessity of being zealous towards yourself first?

4. Why did Jonathan Edwards call Christian zeal "a sweet flame"?

5. How can one stir up and maintain zeal in one's soul?

6. How should zeal for the Lord affect how a worker conducts himself at his job?

Chapter 59

1. How do the Puritans teach us to focus on Christ?

2. What are three important ways to have proper biblical balance in preaching?

3. How did the Puritans see catechism as a means of reaching out to young people, families, and outsiders?

4. What especially made the Puritans great preachers?

5. What three Puritan books can especially help us to respond well to trials?

6. How did the Puritans teach us to fight pride and grow in dependence?

Chapter 60

1. Why was life in Puritan England not easy?

2. What were the strengths of the Puritans?

3. What did the son of Thomas Goodwin say about his father? How is this a model for all Christians, and especially ministers?

4. Do you agree that "the very best theologians the church has produced have been pastors and preachers"? Why?